To Julius Squeezer

Endpapers: Elaphe guttata, *the corn snake, by Ken Lucas at Steinhart Aquarium.*

Title page: Elaphe obsoleta spiloides, *by Ken Lucas at Steinhart Aquarium.*

1.
Snakes as pets

Why do people keep snakes? Those who do consider them far more fascinating than any other pet. They laugh at the innate fear of snakes that lies deep in most of us, a fear that some say dates back to the Garden of

Cuban racer, Alsophis angulifer, *by H. Hansen, Aquarium Berlin.*

Western shovelnosed snake, Chionactis occipitalis, *a very specialized desert burrower. Photo by Richard Holland.*

Eden and Eve's encounter with the serpent. There is no denying that through the ages the snake has always been a symbol of magic and mystery, and even today there are cults that worship it. But there is no sensible reason to fear them.

Collecting snakes in the field can be highly instructive as well as healthful. While hunting them it is impossible not to become interested in other animals and plants and in the principles of ecology—the science that deals with the mutual relations between living things and their environments.

Observing the snake's pattern of behavior can also be rewarding. Seeing how he eats, sleeps, and grows by

Once a very popular pet, the eastern indigo snake, Drymarchon corais, *is now protected in the United States. Photo courtesy American Museum of Natural History.*

Elaphe situla, *the European leopard snake, is a dead ringer for the American corn snake. Photo by Dr. K. Knaack.*

shedding his skin can only add to your interest in this hobby. Many amateur snake collectors have made important contributions to the field of herpetology, the branch of zoology dealing with reptiles and amphibians.

Snakes are easy pets to keep. All they require is a small cage or tank, a light bulb and its accompanying heat, food, and a little care. They are clean, quiet pets, and they need to be fed only once or twice a week. No noise, no walking in cold weather required, and very little cleaning.

One of the most highly prized of North American snakes is the Trans-Pecos rat snake, Elaphe subocularis, *of central Texas. It is difficult to collect and thus fetches a high price when available, and it does fairly well in the hands of a skilled keeper. Photo by Ken Lucas at Steinhart Aquarium.*

Two interesting rarities. Above is the oddly marked *Elapomorphus bilineatus* of South America, a small rear-fanged species. Photo by Dr. M. Freiberg. Below is the green rat snake, *Elaphe triaspis, a Mexican and Central American species that sometimes crosses the border into Arizona and New Mexico. Photo by Robert Holland.*

2.
Something about snakes

There are about 2,100 species of snakes in the world. There are over 100 different kinds (species) in the United States and Canada—fewer than 20 of which are poisonous—and there are over 300 different species in

Heterodon nasicus, *the western hognosed snake. Photo by Ken Lucas at Steinhart Aquarium.*

Mexico. By these figures you can readily see that there are many more snakes in the tropics than there are in the more temperate zones.

Belonging to the suborder Serpentes of the class Reptilia snakes are distinguished by a legless, elongated body covered with scales. These scales are actually horny folds of skin overlapping one another like shingles on a roof. Those on the head are enlarged to provide protection for the delicate bone structure there. While their eyes lack movable eyelids, each is covered by a clear scale, the brille, which they shed along with their skin. Snakes have no external ears, and most of them have only one elongated lung.

Snakes have adapted themselves to greatly different en-

No, this is not a cobra. Neck-spreading occurs in many unrelated snakes. This is Hydrodynastes gigas *of South America, the water cobra, a non-venomous species. Photo by Dr. M. Freiberg.*

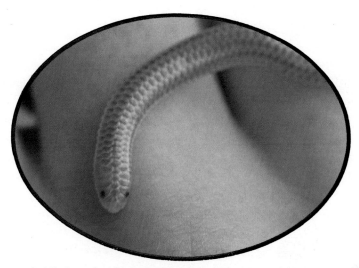

A blind snake, Leptotyphlops humilis, *one of the most primitive of snakes—some scientists consider it to actually be a lizard! Photo by Ken Lucas at Steinhart Aquarium.*

vironments. Most of them are terrestrial, but some are burrowers, other tree-dwellers; still others are aquatic or even marine. Strictly speaking, they are not cold-blooded animals. Like fishes they take on the temperature of their surroundings. They cannot regulate their own body temperature internally but must depend upon the temperature of their environment, although like other reptiles they can control their body temperature fairly well through behavior, such as basking. This type of animal is called poikilothermic. Snakes cannot exist where the subsoil is permanently frozen, though a few species range north almost to the Arctic circle.

As for evolution, snakes have left us very little in the way of fossil records. Scientists believe they evolved from lizards and lost their legs somewhere along the way. Snake vertebrae are common fossils since the Cretaceous (the period when dinosaurs were at their peak), and many fossil species have been described.

Snakes in myth and religion

Snakes have left us untold myths and legends that go far back into the dim mists of history, and they have played an important part in man's religion.

In Mexico the Aztecs worshipped a serpent god named Quetzalcoatl, the Master of Life. In a sixteenth-century Mexican calendar, he is shown swallowing a man. Even today, in northeastern Arizona the Hopi Indians, just as their ancestors did, perform a ritual known as the snake dance. During this ceremony they handle live rattlesnakes. In ancient Egypt one of the divinities was Buto, the snake goddess and protector of the Lower Nile.

In religion, snakes have symbolized both good and evil. There has always been a kind of magic aura associated

Juvenile whipsnake, Masticophis flagellum. *Like the adults of their species, juvenile whipsnakes also have been falsely accused as people-whippers. Photo by Richard Haas.*

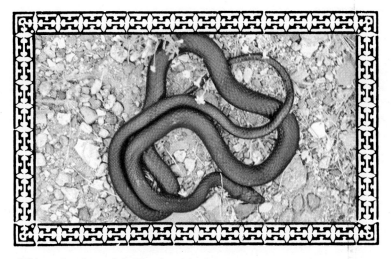

Whipsnakes (an adult Masticophis flagellum *shown here) are greatly feared in some areas. Although they are aggressive biters and will fight determinedly when cornered, they do not "whip" anyone. Photo by Richard Holland.*

with them. Man, in his fear and ignorance, has endowed them with all manner of myths.

One of the most common is that of the snake that when struck breaks into many pieces that then, miraculously, come back together again. The "snake" of this myth is the glass lizard. This lizard has no external legs and grows to about 2 feet in length. More than half of this length is tail. This enables the lizard to slither off leaving his startled captor watching the wriggling tail. The tail and body never reassemble. The lizard grows a new tail over a period of months.

Farmers once thought that there was a kind of snake that would sneak into their barns at night and milk their cows. They named this pretty little kingsnake the milk snake. But if the farmer killed these milk snakes he quickly discovered a sudden increase in the number of mice eating his grain. The farmers quickly learned that

Milk snakes are red, yellow (or white), and black tricolored ringed kingsnakes that feed mostly upon mice and lizards. They have long been accused of stealing milk from cows—and even nursing human mothers— but of course this is totally a myth. Photo of Lampropeltis zonata *by Ken Lucas at Steinhart Aquarium.*

the milk snake did not drink milk but that it did eat mice. Wise farmers now realize the value of these snakes and make them welcome, treating them almost like pets. Snakes do not drink milk if they have water; they cannot digest it.

Snakes are not slimy, although uninformed people may think so. Their scales are dry; it is their lustrous texture that makes them look wet.

Most people, on seeing a snake swimming, immediately assume that it is a poisonous water moccasin. Many picnickers and swimmers have scrambled away in a hurry from innocuous little water snakes. Water moccasins are found throughout the South, but the northernmost part of their range is the Dismal Swamp of Virginia.

Most snakes are not poisonous. Only in Australia are there more poisonous than nonpoisonous snakes.

How snakes move

Even though evolution has cost the snakes their legs, they still manage to get around very well. They do not move, however, as fast as they appear to. The fastest snakes are the whipsnakes and racers of North America. They have been timed at a little over three miles an hour.

Snakes move by means of muscles and belly scales called scutes. These scutes catch on all the rough objects on the ground, and the muscles propel the snake forward. There are three types of locomotion: the inverted "S", caterpillar, and sidewinder. The inverted "S" is the most common. The snake zigzags to pull itself forward. The caterpillar motion is used by the heavier

Garter snakes like this Thamnophis proximus *are not the fastest moving snake species. Photo by J. K. Langhammer.*

snakes like boa constrictors and pythons. The snake moves in a straight line, hunching first the forward part of its body, then the middle, and last the tail. It is the slowest of the three means of locomotion. The sidewinder motion is used only by desert snakes. It enables them to move on loose sand. The head is held up and the snake's body forms an inverted "J".

Sight

Snakes do not have eyelids, but a single clear scale covers their eye. The nocturnal snakes often have elliptical pupils. Snakes active during the day usually have round pupils. None of them can see well beyond 15 feet.

The vipers and pit vipers, such as this tree-dwelling Bothrops nigroviridis, *have vertically elliptical pupils and are strongly adapted to feeding at night. Photo by Dr. S. Minton.*

ɔst colubrids (common snakes) have round pupils and are not especially adapted searching for food at night. This photo of Philodryas burmeisteri *above shows ɛ shape of the eye excellently; photo by H. Piacentini.*

Sex

It takes a professional herpetologist to determine the sex of a snake. The color patterns are the same in male and female. Usually the female's tail is more slender at the base than the male's, because the male has paired hemipenes (copulatory organs) in the base of the tail.

Hearing and smell

Snakes do not have external ears; they are deaf to airborne sounds and human voices. They use their tongues to pick up vibrations in the air. Contrary to public opinion, a snake does not sting with its tongue. The reason that it is flicked in and out is because the tongue is a sensory organ. Located in the roof of a snake's mouth are pits called Jacobson's Organs. The snake collects a

21

sample of air with its tongue and then withdraws it to analyze the sample with these Jacobson's Organs. While a snake cannot hear us talk, it can feel ground vibrations such as those made by our footsteps.

Their sense of smell is keen. Rattlesnakes and other pit vipers not only have this keenly developed sense, they have pits on the sides of their heads that can detect heat. This enables them to find warm-blooded animals for food.

Clearly visible in this photo of the Mojave rattlesnake, Crotalus scutatus, *are its extremely sensitive tongue and the large sensory pit before the eye. Photo by F. J. Dodd, Jr.*

3.
— Selecting your snake —

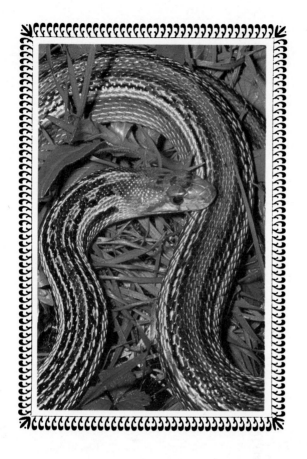

In choosing a snake as a pet, you must first consider the type of food eaten so you will know if you are able to feed it. We are going to divide the snakes into two categories. The first consists of those snakes that prefer to

A striped gopher snake, Pituophis melanoleucus catenifer. *Photo by Ken Lucas at Steinhart Aquarium.*

The California kingsnake, Lampropeltis getulus californiae. *Photo by F. J. Dodd, Jr.*

eat warm-blooded animals, such as the kingsnakes and rat snakes. The second group, including water snakes and garter snakes, are those that eat cold-blooded animals like fishes and frogs.

Snakes that prefer warm-blooded animals will, in captivity, eat mice. If you cannot catch your own mice, they can be purchased in pet shops. Generally speaking, this category makes the better pet. They are easy to handle and seldom make any attempt to bite. If you are squeamish about feeding live mice, get a snake that has been trained to eat frozen mice.

Water snakes and garter snakes can, in captivity, be fed fishes and frogs. Fishes can be purchased easily and stored in the freezer. While this category is easier to feed, there is one serious drawback. Some have nervous dispositions that make them harder to handle. Being high-strung reptiles, they dart about and may attempt to bite. They are also messy to feed and keep clean.

If you are a beginner, we recommend a snake from the mouse-eating category.

MOUSE-EATING SNAKES

Kingsnakes *(Lampropeltis):* The common king snake *(L. getulus)* is a handsome black snake with yellow rings or small spots the length of the body. At maturity it is five to seven feet long. Common kingsnakes range from southern New Jersey to Florida and west to California. They live near water and are frequently found around barns. They kill by constriction. Their diet includes mice, frogs, lizards, and other snakes. They are probably the most gentle and easiest snakes to maintain in captivity. They make a wonderful show, and because of

The blairi *phase of the Mexican kingsnake,* Lampropeltis mexicana. *Photo by Ken Lucas at Steinhart Aquarium.*

their mild behavior they are easy to handle. There are a number of other species of kingsnakes including the milk snakes, coral kings, and gray-banded king. With the possible exception of the milk snake (*L. triangulum*) they all make good pets. They received the name of "king" because of their ability to conquer and eat other snakes, including rattlers and copperheads.

The various species of tricolored (red-black-yellow or white) kings such as the milk snakes and coral kings are especially prized as pets by advanced keepers but they are expensive and often very difficult to keep successfully. Some are protected species.

Boa constrictor *(Boa constrictor):* Boa constrictors come from Mexico and Central and South America. Arboreal (tree-climbing) snakes, they can in the wild grow to be 12 to 14 feet long. Baby boas, which are born

A spectacularly colored specimen of eastern kingsnake, Lampropeltis getulus, *a species that makes an excellent pet if you can feed it mice or snakes. Photo by Ken Lucas at Steinhart Aquarium.*

Drymobius margaritiferus, *the speckled racer, a Mexican and Texas species that is sometimes available but does poorly in captivity. Photo by M. A. del Toro.*

alive, can usually be purchased in pet shops. They are gentle and will take live mice or sparrows readily; they will sometimes eat a piece of beef if it is warmed and moved to simulate life. Boas don't grow as large in captivity as they do in the wild so don't worry about your boa getting to be 14 feet long.

Pilot black snake (*Elaphe obsoleta obsoleta*): The pilot black snake is black with a whitish belly. Babies have a banded pattern. They live in the Northeast, mostly in high rocky places. They make desirable pets for several reasons. Pilots have a mild disposition and will eat well in captivity. They prefer mice but will accept small birds.

Other subspecies of *Elaphe obsoleta* are called rat snakes. They are found over much of the southern U.S. Both adults and young are banded or blotched. Some rat snakes exceed 9 feet in length. Southern subspecies are often nervous and are vicious biters, striking and tearing repeatedly.

Corn snake *(Elaphe guttata):* Corn snakes are probably the most beautiful of the North American snakes. They are gray or orange with red saddles bordered by black. Corn snakes range from southern New Jersey to Florida and west to the Great Plains. The most beautiful speci-

The fox snake, Elaphe vulpina, *is seldom available commercially but can be collected by hobbyists in the Midwest. Photo by J. T. Kellnhauser.*

mens are found in South Carolina, where they grow to their largest size, but Florida also has beautiful specimens. Corn snakes like to climb trees, but they can often be found in deserted old houses and barns. They eat mice, rats, birds, and even young chicks, which they kill by constriction. In captivity, corn snakes make wonderful pets. They are good eaters, accepting mice and birds dead or alive. Corn snakes are a little nervous, so they should not be handled more than necesary al-

ove: *The* "rossalleni" *phase of the black rat snake,* Elaphe obsoleta, *is a
ida form that does well in captivity and can be bred. Photo by J. T. Kelln-
ser.* **Below:** *The Asian* "beauty snake," Elaphe taeniura, *a close relative of
common black rat snake.*

The corn snake, Elaphe guttata, *is one of the most desirable of pet snakes, at least for the more advanced hobbyist. It does well in captivity (but usually prefers live food), is long-lived, colorful, and reproduces well. Photo by Dr. K. Knaack.*

though they seldom bite. Corn snakes are now commonly raised in captivity, and an albino strain is often available at reasonable prices.

Eastern indigo snake *(Drymarchon corais couperi):* The indigo is the largest North American snake. The record so far is almost 10 feet, but the average is 6 feet. Eastern indigo snakes range from South Carolina to Florida and westward to eastern Albama. The eastern indigo is a beautiful satiny black snake. Unlike the other mouse-eating snakes discussed here, the indigo does not kill its prey by constriction. It overpowers it and eats it while it is struggling. They feed on mice, gophers, rabbits, birds, lizards, and other snakes. They are an easy snake to maintain in captivity since they will eat so many different things. Gentle by nature, indigo snakes even seem to show affection for their owners.

Because their habitat has been greatly restricted, eastern indigo snakes are now protected and no longer legally sold. Less colorful tropical cousins are sometimes available, however.

FISH-EATING SNAKES

Water snakes *(Natrix):* Water snakes are found all over the United States east of the Great Plains. They have strongly keeled scales and stout bodies. Their color is on the dull side except for a few southern species that have brightly colored patterns. Water snakes, obviously, are always found near water. They should not, however, be confused with the deadly water moccasin whose large triangular head is sharply distinct from its body. Water moccasins are not found north of the Dismal Swamp in Virginia. Water snakes feed on fishes, frogs, and other amphibians. They kill their prey by simply overpowering it. They are rapacious eaters and can consume large quantities of fish. In captivity they will always take fishes and frogs. However, some have a very nasty disposition and should be handled carefully. They have scent glands, and when annoyed they hiss loudly and emit their scent.

Garter snake *(Thamnophis):* Garter snakes have the most extensive range of any genus of North American snakes. They are found in every mainland state as well as in Alaska and Canada. They have a striped pattern and grow to be 2 to 4 feet long. They are often found in fields but usually near water. They eat fishes, frogs, and earthworms by overpowering them. In captivity they accept fishes readily and will eat earthworms. They are nervous when newly caught and dart about their cages. They are extremely hard to handle then because they will try to bite. They are common and cheap to buy. Once acclimated to captivity they are hardy and become quite tame. These are fine species on which to begin your experiences as a snake-keeper.

Ribbon snakes *(Thamnophis sauritus* and *T. proximus):* Ribbon snakes are widely distributed in the eastern states. While their close relatives the garter snakes live close to ponds, lakes, and streams, ribbon snakes are found more often in fields and near rocky ledges. They have a slim brown to black body with yellow or white lines running its length. Individuals vary greatly from area to area. Ribbon snakes will eat the same kind of food as other garter snakes: worms, frogs, fishes. Like water snakes and garter snakes in general, they give birth to live young in the late summer. The eggs mature within the female and have membranes instead of hard shells.

A juvenile corn snake. Corns are now commonly available that have been bred in captivity, putting no stress on wild populations. Photo by Aaron Norman.

Above: *A head study of the indigo snake,* Drymarchon corais. *Photo by J. T. Kellnhauser.* **Below:** *A young banded water snake,* Natrix sipedon, *one of the most common eastern American snakes. American* Natrix *species are now commonly put in the genus* Nerodia *mostly because they give birth, while Eurasian* Natrix *lay eggs. Photo by F. J. Dodd, Jr.*

In captivity, ribbon snakes accept food readily. They will eat chopped-up fishes, worms, and small frogs. Sometimes they eat slugs and field crickets. But like the garter snakes, they are nervous and take a while to adapt to captivity. While they are hard to handle at first, they do not bite as readily as water snakes and some other garter snakes; they are therefore the most desirable of the three.

Butler's garter snake is an uncommon species with a limited range near the Great Lakes. This albino Thamnophis butleri *is an especially attractive and interesting find. Photo by Jeff Gee.*

4.
Poisonous snakes

No amateur should attempt to keep a poisonous snake or to hunt one. Many professional herpetologists have died from their bites, and even if a poisonous snake's bite isn't lethal, it can cause serious aftereffects.

The water moccasin or cottonmouth, Agkistrodon piscivorus.

Most municipalities have strict laws against keeping poisonous snakes, and one has no right to expose his family or neighbors to such a danger. There are far too many non-poisonous snakes available to make the collecting of poisonous ones worth the terrible risk.

Until recent times about five thousand people died every year in India from the bite of the Indian cobra, krait, and Russell's viper. In South America thousands of barefoot peasants were killed annually by South American pit vipers. We now have antivenins that have cut down on this alarming death rate. Scientists have found a way to make a serum from the blood of horses. This serum is processed and kept by doctors and hospitals for use if there is an emergency.

There are four groups of poisonous snakes in the United States. They are the rattlesnakes, the copperhead, and the cottonmouth water moccasin of the subfamily Crotalinae of the family Viperidae (i.e., pit vipers), and the coral snakes of the Elapidae. The first three groups are highly distinctive and readily identified, but the coral snakes resemble a number of harmless snakes, among them the scarlet snake and the tricolored kingsnakes. If red bands touch yellow bands, the snake is a coral snake and not a kingsnake or scarlet snake.

Expert opinions on treating snakebites vary greatly, some doctors recommending a tourniquet, others ice. If bitten, try to stay calm and get to emergency treatment at once. Few people die of snakebites in the U.S., and few of our 20 or so venomous species will kill a healthy adult even with minimal treatment available.

5.
Getting your snake

There are two ways to get a pet snake: you can go out and catch your own or you can obtain one from a dealer or other enthusiast.

One of the more colorful forms of garter snake, Thamnophis sirtalis concinnus. *Photo by Richard Holland.*

When you buy a snake, be on the lookout for several things. Be sure that the snakes' cages are clean; this will assure you that the dealer has been taking good care of them. Their bodies should have no abrasions and they should, of course, be free of disease.

Finding your own snake is more fun, though often less practical. Certain equipment is needed. You will need a good pair of walking boots, a snake stick (which is a stick about 3 feet long with a blunt hook on the end), and a cloth bag. When you've caught your snake and dropped it into the bag, make a knot in the bag at the top and there is no way your snake can escape if the corner and bottom seams are tight. The cloth permits fresh air to circulate so the snake can breathe.

The best time to collect snakes is in the spring. They have just come out of hibernation then and are moving around during the day. In the East they are usually

The large snakes of the genus Pituophis, *the pine snakes and bull snakes, are found in most states of the U.S. and make excellent pets.* *Photo by Richard Haas.*

The little brown snake or DeKay's ground snake is often very common and will do well in captivity, feeding on small invertebrates of various types, but it is a burrower and not an exciting pet. Photo of Storeria dekayi *by J. K. Langhammer.*

found near water, so always search for them in the vicinity of lakes, ponds, or streams. They can be found hiding under rocks and pieces of wood.

If you are fortunate enough to find a great many snakes in one area, collect only a few. Otherwise you can upset the precious balance of nature that exists there.

Before collecting or even buying a snake, be aware of your local laws. Many states and cities require permits before snakes can be kept as pets. In many states the collecting of snakes is frowned upon, strictly regulated, or even prohibited. The old days of walking into the woods and collecting two or three kingsnakes are largely gone. In fact, many states prohibit the keeping of rat snakes, corn snakes, and kingsnakes because their habitat has been destroyed and the species are threatened.

A magnificent pine snake, Pituophis melanoleucus. *It is one of the most spectacular of North American snakes, reaching a length of over 8 feet and having a very aggressive hissing display. This specimen, photographed by Ken Lucas at Steinhart Aquarium, is probably the northern pine snake.*

6.
Selecting the cage

Snakes require a relatively small cage in proportion to their size. The smallest varieties can live in a cage that measures 20 x 12 x 12 inches. This is, roughly, the size of a ten-gallon fish tank. Larger, more active snakes require relatively larger cages.

The European green racer, Coluber viridiflavus. *Courtesy Dr. D. Terver, Nancy Aquarium, France.*

Fish tanks are quite suitable and readily obtainable. Most pet shops now carry stainless steel mesh tops to fit the various sizes of aquaria. You should have one of these. Pet shops also sell reflectors for incandescent bulbs. One of these will light the tank and generate the necessary heat. A 50-watt bulb can be used in an aquarium. The larger the tank, the higher the wattage needed, within reason.

You can build your own cage if you are handy, but it will probably cost more than a fish tank. It should have a glass front, but the other three sides can be solid. The top is the door; screening (attached under the frame) is placed there to allow ventilation. A light-socket should be wired into the cage at the top of the back wall for illumination. The bulb will also give off enough heat to keep your snake warm during cold weather. A 60-watt bulb is about right; never use one of more than 75

A Sinaloan milk snake, Lampropeltis triangulum, *living the life of luxury in a cage fitted with all the modern conveniences. Photo by Jeff Gee.*

A cat-eye snake, Leptodeira annulata, *being kept under the most Spartan of conditions, just newspaper and a few bits of wood for hiding places in an all-glass tank. Photo by J. T. Kellnhauser.*

watts. The door or lid should be secured with a good lock. Snakes are great escape artists, so when building your cage make sure that there are no openings. If there are, your snake will be sure to find them and the search is on!

Fish tanks have one great advantage: when you find mites (as you certainly will sooner or later) you will have to sterilize the cage. Sterilizing a fish tank is easier than sterilizing a cage. The tank need only be washed with water and ammonia; a wooden cage would have to be repainted.

All snakes should be kept dry. Even water snakes and garter snakes do not need water to swim in. The water dish that is placed in the cage is all the water that they will need.

Gravel should be spread on the bottom. The medium grade sold for most aquaria is the best. Wash and dry it to get the dust out before using it. Spread the gravel about an inch deep over the bottom. When the snake soils the cage, remove the excrement. The gravel itself should be changed about every two months; this will keep the cage always looking clean.

Professional herpetologists and amateurs with large collections usually use newspaper on the bottoms of their cages. Although newspapers do not look as nice as gravel, they make cage cleaning easy because when soiled they can be thrown away.

Snakes are by nature secretive and they will want a place to hide. If you are using gravel, arrange a few

A female indigo snake with 11 freshly laid eggs on the vermiculite on which they will be hatched. Many snakes can now be raised in captivity. Photo by Jeff Gee.

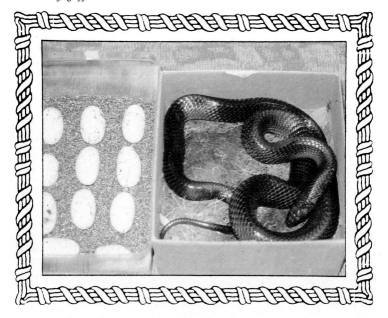

Small, colorful snakes such as the ringneck snake, Diadophis punctatus, *are usually very secretive. If you put them in a cage with many hiding places you will never see them, but if you don't give them hiding places they are stressed and will not do well. Photo by J. K. Langhammer.*

rocks to make a cave, or put a rounded piece of bark in the cage. If you are using newspaper, put in a box with a hole cut in its side. A cigar box is just about the right size for many snakes.

Branches and rocks make fine ornaments. Tree-dwelling snakes will want a branch to coil on. Potted plants and cacti can be added to make the cage more attractive, although they usually do not thrive in a terrarium. Most snakes like to have a flat basking rock under the light; often they will spend much of the day there soaking in the heat.

The desert hooknosed snake, Gyalopion quadrangularis, *barely crosses the border into Arizona from Mexico and is considered a quite rare species. A strict desert-dweller and burrower, it reminds one of a small hognosed snake. Rare species such as this are usually kept only by specialists. Photo by Ken Lucas at Steinhart Aquarium.*

7.
Feeding your snake

A snake devours its food whole. Its teeth are small and are curved backward. All of them are about the same

A hognosed snake, Heterodon platyrhinos, *eating a toad. Photo by F. J. Dodd, Jr.*

size except in the poisonous snakes, where the front teeth are enlarged to enable the snake to eject it venom. (Hognose snakes and some other species have enlarged back teeth.) A snake's jaws are hinged a way that enables it to open the mouth wider than in almost any other animal. When the snake has caught its prey, the food is forced into the mouth by literally scooping in the animal.

Snakes kill their prey by three methods: constriction, overpowering, and injection of poison.

When a snake kills by constriction it tightens its coils around the prey until it suffocates. This is faster than you might think—a mouse is dead in ten seconds. Those snakes that overpower their prey often devour it

Mammal-eaters such as this Oxybelis fulgidus *are often easier to handle, as mice are always available and most mammal-eaters will take frozen and thawed food. Photo by Dr. M. Freiberg.*

Those species (such as Mastigdryas bifossatus, *shown here) that eat frogs and other cold-blooded animals have the problem that their food is often available only seasonally. Photo by Dr. M. Freiberg.*

while it is still struggling; garter snakes and indigo snakes eat this way.

Poisonous snakes have the most efficient method. They inject venom into the animal killing it instantly. The process works so well that the venom starts breaking down the animal for easy digestion before it is completely swallowed. There are two types of poison: hemotoxic venom attacks the heart and blood vessels; neurotoxic venom attacks the nerves and is much more deadly. Cobras and coral snakes have neurotoxic venom, vipers hemotoxic venom, as a general rule.

Watching a snake eat is fascinating. They can swallow animals larger than their heads, always eating them whole. Their backward curving teeth cannot chew the food, but they are very efficient at hooking it into the throat.

The black-necked garter snake, Thamnophis cyrtopsis, *occurs in the south western United States and is not as tied to water as the more typical garter snakes Photo by Richard Holland.*

Pet snakes are not always easy to feed. Garter snakes and water snakes are probably the easiest. They will eat fish, and fishes can always be kept stored in your freezer. Any kind of fish at all will do. Cut it into strips that your snake can swallow and feed about twice a week. Garter snakes will readily eat earthworms. During the spring and summer these will make a welcome change in their diet. They should be fed twice a week. Water snakes like frogs.

Mouse-eating snakes pose some problems for the novice. While garter snakes and water snakes will always accept food in captivity, this is not true of mouse-eating snakes. Knowing the likes and dislikes of your particular snake is important in keeping it healthy.

When you have put your newly acquired snake into its cage, do not offer food for at least a week. Let the snake first become accustomed to its new environment. The first few days will be spent investigating the cage, seeking means of escape. Make certain that the cage is secure. Give a bowl of water immediately. Snakes can go without food for months (but shouldn't!) but they must always have water.

After a week, see if the snake will eat. Purchase a mouse from the pet shop and put it in the cage. The late afternoon is the best feeding time because by then the snake has warmed up. Snakes must always be kept warm or they will have no appetite.

If your snake has adapted to its new environment, he will take the mouse readily. Sometimes he will just look interested. If this happens leave the mouse in the cage for about two hours; then if still uneaten take it out. During the night a snake becomes sluggish and sometimes a mouse will be able to gnaw on him. Snakes have

The western patchnosed snake, Salvadora hexalepis, *is a racer-like snake of the western American deserts that hunts mostly at night; it usually is too nervous to dwell in captivity. Photo by F. J. Dodd, Jr.*

been killed this way by mice and rats.

Remember too that your snake may never have seen a white mouse; he is used to the more natural colors of field mice and rats. If your snake constantly refuses white mice try one of the other colors available. Hamsters are often considered too vicious to be fed to the average snake.

Boa constrictors and kingsnakes are the best feeders. The average-sized snake should be fed one mouse a week; the larger specimens (over 5 feet) two or more.

Many snakes will adapt well to frozen foods that have been thawed. They feed more by scent and body temperature of the prey than its appearance. Many pet shops that sell snakes also sell frozen baby mice ("pinkies") and baby chicks. If your snake will eat these, they will provide a convenient and always available source of food—without regrets about having to kill one animal to feed another.

8.
— Helping your snake —

In order to grow, snakes must shed their skin every few months depending on their age, environment, and feeding habits. In nature they have no trouble shedding; in captivity they may.

An albino garter snake, Thamnophis sirtalis sirtalis, *from Iowa. Photo by Jeff Gee.*

When your snake's scales begin to lose their luster and the eyes cloud to a milky white or blue your pet is getting ready to shed. The eyes will clear just before the shedding starts. Moisture then becomes very important. Put into the cage a water bowl large enough for the snake to completely immerse himself and fill it full of water (allowing for displacement by the snake's bulk).

If there are no rough objects in the cage, provide a rock for the snake to rub against; the skin will come off eas-

The racers and whipsnakes, Coluber *and* Masticophis, *are large, nervous snakes that seldom do well in captivity and often never settle down.* Photo by Ken Lucas at Steinhart Aquarium.

ily. Sometimes it will come off in one piece, making an interesting curio that may be kept with your collection.

Snakes often do not shed properly, and this is when your help is needed. The clear scales that cover his eyes may not be shed correctly; this can lead to an infection. Simply remove this scale with a pair of blunt-tipped tweezers. If your snake does not have enough moisture

Top: *A typical specimen of the common eastern garter snake,* Thamnophis sirtalis sirtalis. *Many garter snakes calm down very rapidly in captivity and make excellent pets, although freshly captured specimens may be bad biters. Most garter snakes will eventually adapt to almost any type of food. Photo by J. K. Langhammer.* **Bottom:** *The sharp-tailed snake of the Pacific Northwest,* Contia tenuis, *is a secretive little species that feeds on many types of lizards and invertebrates. It is not well-known and seldom is kept in captivity. Photo by Ken Lucas at Steinhart Aquarium.*

when preparing to shed, it will be in trouble. Dryness and an adhering skin bother the snake because it cannot breathe or move easily with a layer of dead skin enveloping the body.

To remedy this condition, punch holes in the lid of a large jar. Punch them from the underside up so there won't be any sharp points on which he can injure himself. Put in a damp towel or wad of paper towels and let your snake stay in it for three days. It will then be able to shed its skin with ease.

When the dead skin has been shed, you will find the new skin exceptionally beautiful. Indigo snakes and boa constrictors, for example, reflect the light, and their colors after shedding are exquisite.

9.
Snake diseases

In captivity, diseases and parasites are far more dangerous to your pet than when it was living wild. Many parasites can be checked by the snake in the field by chang-
ing its living place and varying the diet.

The Mexican kingsnake, Lampropeltis mexicana, *color
phase* blairi. *Photo by R. W. Applegate.*

One of the most serious diseases to infect snakes is "mouth rot." This is caused by a bacteria that kills muscle and bone tissue in the mouth and respiratory tract. When adding a snake to your collection always examine its mouth. Snakes attacked by this disease have creamy-textured white patches in their mouths. Sometimes the teeth have been eaten away and the mouth has a foul smell.

Mouth rot is hard to get rid of, and it is a contagious disease. Isolate the animal immediately and buy an appropriate antibiotic (tetracycline, ampicillin) at the pet shop. Give the antibiotic, following directions on the package, until at least two days after the infection is no longer visible. Usually a snake with mouth rot stops eat-

Egg-laying is a delicate time for some snakes. The eggs may get stuck in the female's reproductive tract, resulting in death of the specimen. Maintaining proper humidity and temperature in the cage should prevent problems of this sort. Photo of Hypsiglena torquata *by J. K. Langhammer.*

Virtually all snakes should be kept relatively dry, even semi-aquatic species such as this mangrove snake, Boiga irregularis. *Keeping any snake wet all the time will result in bacterial and fungal infections. Photo by J. T. Kellnhauser.*

ing. After treatment has been given, try to get him to eat. If he eats there is a good chance that he is cured. Sponging the mouth with mild solutions of Merthiolate or hydrogen peroxide may speed the cure.

Snakes purchased during the cold winter months are in danger of developing bad colds that can lead to death. Snakes with colds keep their heads up and are constantly opening their mouths. Their nasal passages are clogged. They refuse food. The best treatment for colds are antibiotics available from your pet shop (tetracycline) or veterinarian. Follow instructions on the package. When the congestion goes away and the mouth stays closed, the snake should take food.

There are many parasites that infest snakes, although only a few are dangerous...to him, not to you—you cannot "catch" them. Mites pose the biggest problem.

They are tiny arachnids the size of a pinpoint. They congregate around the snake's eyes and under his belly scales. They are black to red and can be seen quite clearly. They suck blood and if not checked can cause severe blood loss. They may also serve as hosts for protozoan parasites and may lead to fungal infections.

Treatment must be thorough or the mites will reinfest the snake. The cage must be completely disinfected along with all its ornaments. Use ammonia. Throw away all sand and gravel and replace it with new. If the cage is wooden, repaint it. You must work fast if you have more than one snake or the mites will spread to the rest of your collection.

Mites on the snakes can be killed by drowning (not very effective), silica gel powder (Dri-Die 67)—which may be harmful to small snakes, and insecticides such as DDVP (Vapona, pest strips). It is best to talk to your pet shop dealer or vet before starting any treatment.

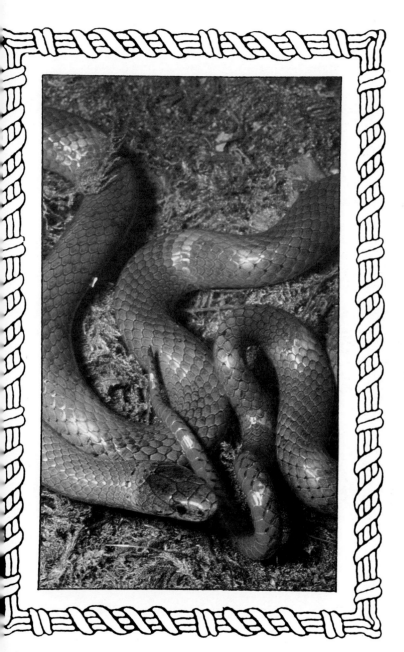

ringneck snake, Diadophis punctatus, *at its best. Photo by Ken Lucas at einhart Aquarium.*